Forged Through The Fire

4 Steps to Transform Adversity Into Opportunity

D'Leene DeBoer

TABLE OF CONTENTS

"Making the decision to have a child - it is momentous. It is to decide forever to have your heart go walking outside your body."

~ Elizabeth Stone

Acknowledgments

I sit here feeling so incredibly humbled and insignificant, in the best way possible, when I think of all the people I want to acknowledge. It takes a village and I'm so very blessed to have the one I do. There really aren't enough words to capture the level of love, gratitude, and admiration I have for everyone who has loved, supported, and mentored me along the way. Thank you isn't enough for every single person who has walked with me at any point, for any amount of time, on this journey. I wouldn't be who I am now or where I am now without all of you. I didn't do this alone, and I am thankful and blessed beyond measure. Thank you all so much, so very much.

James, my amazing husband. You choose me and have been with me through so much. Thanks to you, I'm not just surviving, I'm thriving in a relationship I didn't know was possible. Thank you for pushing me to go farther and to places I never would have without you by my side. You have jumped in and harnessed up with me for every moment as we build our vision together. Your support, commitment, love, honor, and dad jokes have been my safe place, so I can confidently take on any challenge that comes. I choose you every day....and so we dance, today, tomorrow, and always. I love you MORE!

Brennan, you are a living miracle and blessing. I'm so incredibly thankful and blessed I get to be your mom. Thank you for your incredible love, thoughtfulness, courage, and support. I love who you are and who you choose to BE. Getting to be your mom is my biggest honor and my most amazing accomplishment. I promise to always fight for you and give you the life and opportunities you deserve. Watching you build your dreams and be the loving, brilliant human you are is a privilege I do not take for granted. I love you to the moon and back. Also, I love you MORE!

Rylan and Kearnan, I'm so thankful to be your mom. I wish so much I could be watching you grow up and BE all of the things only you would BE. I know I wouldn't be who I am today without getting to be your mom and love you the way only a mother can. You first made me a mom, and it is my most cherished title. You are loved and thought of every single day...every single day.

"You gain strength, courage and confidence by every experience in which you really stop to look fear in the face. You are able to say to yourself, 'I have lived through this horror. I can take the next thing that comes along.' You must do the thing you think you cannot do."

~ Eleanor Roosevelt

The Spark

Life doesn't always go as planned...I learned this the hard way. I even dug my heels in against the direction the universe was sending me, so the universe got louder.

In the blink of an eye, my entire life changed, and I was thrust onto a path I could no longer resist. When I closed my eyes, I was 23 years old and 39 weeks pregnant with my first son, Rylan, sitting in the passenger side of the car reading my book "Birthing Without Fear". When I opened them, it was a week later, I was in the hospital, surrounded by friends and family whose faces told me they weren't sure they would ever get me back. My little '89 Toyota Corolla was T-boned by a cement truck at approx 50mph. The car was wrapped around me, leading to an extended extraction time, increasing my mortality rate. Thankfully, an amazing trauma surgeon heard my case called in, and an incredible trauma team prepared for my arrival. They weren't sure I would survive, and I beat the odds. There is so much more and I will save those details for another time. They aren't the focus of this book.

Waking up was strange as I didn't know how much time had passed and had no conscious memories from the previous week. I don't have a conscious memory of being told that my son had died, but I knew he was. The way my heart protected itself was just feeling he was in the nursery while I recovered, and this was all just a nightmare. My sister crawled into the hospital bed with me and held me while the reality I could no longer hide from sank in. She gave me a safe space. There was no judgement, no shame, no guilt, no blame. She never made me feel like I was grieving "wrong" by trying to "make me feel better" with words. She simply held me and held space for my heartbreak. I love her so much and I'm so incredibly lucky she gave me that gift.

As the days unfolded, I would learn how I died multiple times and my emergency and trauma team fought diligently to save my life. They never gave up on me, and I am so grateful. I would learn that I lost my uterus, due to rupture. My future of having children was unclear as my one remaining ovary was so badly damaged from the car accident it might not work. My medical team was preparing me for early menopause just in case it didn't start working again. I would learn that it was unclear how long rehabilitation would take, or if I would return to my prior level of function, because of the extent of my injuries. I would learn that I could buy a small house with the cost of my portion of the medical debt.

I learned how to cope with the plenitude of things this accident brought to my life and it allowed me to be here, writing this book, today. It took me a long time to fully accept what happened and to be grateful for the lessons it taught me. In fact, I dug my heels in against the learning because my traumatized heart thought that meant being thankful I lost my son. I didn't see how I was holding myself back as a result and putting my life on hold. I believed I was being a "good mom"...

Then, one year later, after what was a successful IVF transfer with a surrogate...I lost my second son, Kearnan, at 6 months gestation. I collapsed onto the cold, hard, tile floor in the ultrasound room when I saw no movement and no heart beating. The loss was devastating. It was like second impact syndrome, but for life. I couldn't believe this was happening again. My brain and heart were trying to understand why I was being punished, because I was not aware of the deeper lessons in all of this. I was just a heartbroken mother who had to bury my babies. They are, side-by-side, in a cemetery called "Baby Land". How do you tell a mother to move on with her children gone? I didn't know then that wasn't the right thought or question. I still had more important lessons to learn before I started paying attention to what I needed to learn, so I could grow.

A fire ignited in my heart and just wanted to live, love and be happy. I started paying attention to some of the lessons, and 1 year later, my son, Brennan, was born. I heard him crying as I entered the birthing center. As I walked into the nursery, he turned his head and stopped crying. The nurse said, "He knows you're his parents". I got to breastfeed him and I remember just repeating "This is what mommies do". I sat there holding my baby, thinking I was finally on the other side. Nothing else mattered. I was so in love with my son and I would be the best mom, no matter what it required of me.

There were still more lessons, and I won't go into all of them in this book. Just know that lessons keep repeating themselves until we learn them. I learned I'm more stubborn than I ever thought because the universe was working overtime to get me to wake up. I don't recommend it so don't do what I did, learn from my mistakes.

"Our greatest glory is not in never falling, but in rising every time we fall."

~ *Confucius*

The Flame

It's fair to say I was a mess and struggling. I did my best to hold everything together, especially myself. If I fell apart, the house of cards would crumble. I tried so many things on my journey to happiness and peace. None of it worked individually. It was the combination and years of practice that brought it all together, so I could get to the other side.

A huge turning point for me was when one of my best friends took her life. I was in the middle of a traumatic and vile divorce, that has been more than 7 years of litigation led by my ex, and all I could do to was fight for what was best for my son. She was there for me in so many ways. When I was given the news, I went into shock and then had a complete breakdown. It was the first time in my life I couldn't get myself back up. The only things I could make myself do were to take care of my son. It was the first time in my life I knew something close to what depression must feel like for people.

Even in my despair, I knew that if this went on, my life would spiral out of control and I wouldn't be able to give Brennan the life he deserves. I picked up the phone and reached out to a dear friend of mine, who is a life coach and energy healer. I told her I needed help and was in an immense hole of despair. Her coaching and energy work turned my life around, and I am forever grateful to her for unleashing my spirit. She helped me realize how much my heart wanted to help people in this way, and she has been a great example and mentor for me.

I have had many people over the years tell me I need to write a book because I have been through so much and come out so strong. The reality was I didn't have a conscious awareness of what I was doing. I felt like there was no other choice than to keep moving forward. I have done many steps, programs and workbooks that have given me insight into what I was doing accidentally that helped me persevere over the years. What I have been able to do that helped the most is a Root Cause Analysis (Sometimes my geekdom slips out #sorrynotsorry). I'm a process improvement geek. I love it. One thing we do in process improvement is we look at the root cause of an issue. In me doing this for personal development, I did what's called a "Retrospective Analysis". I looked for the common threads/themes to find some root sources. Identifying the roots of transforming adversity into opportunity made handling tough experiences much simpler. The Forged Method was born and is getting results so much faster for myself and others.

One of the key links to what holds people back is from our brain. Our brains are masters at avoiding pain, so our subconscious influences how we deal with any painful experience. Let's use fire as an example. When there is fire, we avoid touching it, so we don't get burned. If we accidentally touch it, we pull away quickly. If we are fire walking, we do it quickly because sitting in it means getting burned and possibly death. Painful experiences are no different with how it feels to lean in/sit in the fire with the pain, feelings, thoughts and emotions. We pull away as quickly as possible; there are many ways people do this. They include food, alcohol, drugs, aggression, control, authoritarianism, and more. A book everyone should read that touches more on this is "Adult Children of Alcoholics" by Dr. Janet G. Woititz, resources list at the back of the book. You can replace alcoholics with any form of abuse or neglect and it explains why humans are the way they are, why they respond as they do, and allows us to hold more compassion and grace for ourselves and others. This should be a required read in high school and college in my opinion, it's that important.

As humans, we are masters at avoiding pain, particularly emotional pain. What we don't see is that the key to healing and happiness is through the pain, through the fire. Sitting with it, feeling it, being aware of it, accepting it, letting it soften us, and knowing how to work with it. The only way out is through. When we avoid pain, we hold ourselves back from anything that resembles risk of pain because we don't have evidence that the pain doesn't lead to death. We like to believe we are more evolved than we are; being aware of the hold our primal brain has over us is one way to gain momentum in the right direction.

The Forged Method has been that right direction and I'm thankful I finally have the understanding to put it into words for others to benefit from too. Not every tool works for every person or every situation. However, every time you try, you will gain more understanding and have lasting benefit from that knowledge. You can learn something impactful from every tool and it's worth it to return to yourself, reclaim your freedom and power. I can't guarantee everything will be rainbows and unicorns by the end of this journey. Also, can't guarantee that it won't be. I can tell you it's worth diving in and that you will be better for the new lenses to look through. You are worth taking the time to learn from you, and only you can provide that to yourself.

Something you should know about me before we move forward is that I'm a human golden retriever. I love people and it fills my heart getting to be in community with others. So, when I say you matter to me, I mean it from the depths of my soul. Thank you for being here and for trying this out. My respect and admiration to you on this journey.

Thank you so much and let's get FORGED!

"You have to be forged through fire in order to earn the right to say that you can do hard things."

The Fire And Being Forged

I heard this quote, and it hit my soul hard because this is the work I have been doing to get to the other side. I have searched trying to find who said it, and my results have come up empty since I'm not sure how it was said exactly, this is my version of it. All I know is I want to thank whoever said it because it helped me put all the pieces together. I am so grateful I heard it and that was a message from the universe to put me here, in this moment, sharing with all of you.

I will walk you through my method step-by-step so you can do what took me years in less than three months. What feeds my soul is helping others live their best life and seeing them happy. I was afraid to write a book for a long time for so many reasons...one being that I didn't believe I was worthy of my soul's calling to do this work. Not only that, I thought, who am I to write a book and share with people how to heal when I'm still healing? What I discovered is that, from my perspective, the healing is never "done". The wounds are always there. Our lived experiences are always with us. We can learn how to build ourselves from and with them, not be destroyed by them. I continue to do this work on the different layers. I have a plan when I slide back into old beliefs about not being worthy, so I can live out my dream and my life's purpose. I'm so excited to share this information with every single one of you.

The process of forging is a powerful analogy for transforming painful experiences. In order to be forged, the metal must sit in the fire to get hot enough for molding to be possible. Once the metal is hot enough to be molded, someone can manually shape it into anything or cast it into specific tools to be used in building, living, and so on. Let's look deeper into this and how it relates to our painful experiences in life.

I know for many we can wear our mental and emotional well-being heavily in our physical body. Do not, for a moment, underestimate how unresolved mental and emotional pain from our lived experiences can cause actual physical pain. Behind every illness, injury, and/or disability is a DIS-EASE component. Our mental and emotional well-being is not separate from our physical well-being. There is a lot of supporting research on this and a powerful book is "The Body Keeps the Score" by Dr. Bessel van der Kolk. At the end of this book, I will list many resources so you don't need to write this down or shift your attention from the work you're doing at this moment. Know that if you are experiencing physical struggles, this work will support you too. I say this because I have had people tell me they don't need to do this work, they just need surgery or some medical resolution. Although that can be a part of it, be willing to be surprised at how the ways you physically heal when you heal your mental and emotional.

Now, in order to be forged from our experiences, we must sit in the fire until we are "hot" enough to be molded. We can't live in the fire because eventually there would be nothing left. It is part of what happens in depression. However, if we sit in the pain, fully experience it, ground it, and shift it, then we will be "hot" enough to be molded. What we do in the molding process is vital because we can either be destroyed by the fire or built by it; this will have permanent results, so make them what you dream of, and don't hold back.

An important part of being forged is having instructions and being taught. Most of us don't grow up with this training or guidance. In fact, many of our parents didn't either, and then we grow up coping for them as well. More on that at another time, I digress. In the next section, I will guide you through the Forged Method with examples and there is a workbook as well, so you can start practicing. I have divided the steps up and explain each one to ensure you will gain success with the tools I'm providing here. Having spent most of my life, until now, living on a tight budget, I am always grateful for any resource that is free or affordable for me and helpful. I don't want to leave anyone behind. We all move forward together. Everyone wins when we unite and help each other. I believe in a world of unity, connection, love, and trust.

"Be built by the fire not destroyed by it."

~ *D'Leene DeBoer*

The Forged Method

The Forged Method is a cognitive and heart-centered approach to leverage the FIRE so you can BE FORGED.

The 4-Step Forged Method:

1. Awareness
2. Acceptance
3. Action Plan
4. Anchoring

These four steps work together to maximize your transformation, and work together so you can build yourself through the fire, not be destroyed by it.

You can take control of your life by following these steps, and without all four, the cycle you are in will persist. If you don't use all four in the correct order, then you will remain stuck and hurting.

The order and all four steps work together to transform adversity into opportunity, so that you can be built by the fire, not destroyed by it. If you try to skip to Acceptance without achieving Awareness, then you aren't clear on exactly what it is you're accepting, and nothing moves forward. If you go through Awareness and skip Acceptance, then the Action Plan and Anchoring will remain in a victim, disempowered mindset. As a result, transformation cannot occur. Skipping the Action Plan means a backslide with no rebuilding. If you decide to skip the Anchoring, then you will have some changes, and it will be a one step forward, two steps back cycle. While it may be fun in cha-cha, it's not a pattern we want to repeat in life.

I will outline each step in the next section and talk about the exercises in the, free downloadable, workbook that pair with each section. I will take you through the FIRE tool and how to use it so that you can be FORGED, not destroyed. You deserve to see your strength and the power of your lived experience, and this will get you there. Download the workbook at www.dleenedeboer.com

The FIRE tool:

F – Face the experience
I – Investigate emotions
R – Reflect on triggers
E – Empower yourself

This tool is in the workbook and shows you how you use the FIRE in the Awareness Step to be FORGED.

I listed resources at the back of the book that I still use and add to, so I can remain anchored. These resources will help you continue your journey in strength, love, and happiness. The workbook is something you can use over and over for each layer of growth. We are complex and just like layers of an onion we pull back one to uncover the next and repeat the healing process. This work is never "done". We are constantly being shaped and creating ourselves. The Forged Method allows us to be in charge of how that happens and who we become.

Now let's dive into the Forged Method and start getting FORGED!

"Hope is the thing with feathers that perches in the soul."

~ Emily Dickinson

Step 1: Awareness

AWARENESS ~ The Spark: The first step to making change happen is awareness. "What does that mean?", you may ask. How do we fix a problem if we don't see/have awareness there is a problem? It also means diving into your painful experiences and bringing light to them and how they affect your thoughts, emotions, motivations, and life. Being "Aware" of your experiences has more to it than one might think. Sure, they are our experiences, so we know them firsthand. However, do you remember that little detail about how our primal brain is so effective in avoiding pain? Well, that primal brain will block out different parts of our painful experiences or change them altogether to protect us from what it thinks of as death. This detail, our brains block it out, while our bodies remember, our hearts remember...

Our body doesn't respond to emotional pain any differently than it does to physical pain or threat. If we experience a breakup, for example, our body can literally feel like it's dying. When our body feels like it's dying, our primal brain jumps in trying to be the hero to shift us out of the experience, so we don't "die". Super helpful, right? Not really, since being open to love and living a full life means there will be pain. Shifting out of the emotional pain prematurely shuts down our ability to reflect, understand, and learn from an experience. The universe and our subconscious then work together, recreating the same types of experiences until we learn from them. You see why the cycle repeats? Let's end that here and now.

In order to reach full awareness, you must sit in the FIRE and get "HOT". I know this sounds incredibly uncomfortable, and it is, but you know what? Nothing that involves growth or success is comfortable, so I'm going to teach you how to be comfortable being uncomfortable. I'm going to help you teach your brain that you're not going to die from emotional pain, and give it the evidence it needs to reprogram its response to emotional pain.

This was an area I struggled with after being molested as a child. I was molested from the time I was about 7yo, what I can remember, until I was 9yo because my parents surrounded us with not so good people. Then, because of jerk hormones that weren't even invited, I started developing breasts when I was 9yo and was a C cup by the time I was 10yo. I started binding my breasts, wearing big and very baggy clothes. I stopped swimming or doing anything that might show my body, and I did this until I was 15 years old.

What changed on a random day when I was 15yo that clued me into gaining awareness? I was watching TV and flipping through the channels when, by chance, I stopped at one. This was the universe leading me because there was nothing exciting about it. It was a simple scene with two women on a boat paddling away from some female oppressive place. One says to the other, "I don't want to die hating the day that I was born a girl and always wondering why I was punished so badly". This one statement changed my life. It was the spark to the fire. All of the emotions and the pain of being molested as a child flooded me. I had been repressing the pain for so long and was completely unaware that it was ruling my life. I was binding my breasts and hiding my body to avoid unwanted attention and the pain that comes with it. By reliving this pain and beginning to fully sit with it, being in the FIRE with it, I could begin to shift. I could now reflect on what happened and not feel like a victim to it or to the experience. I stopped feeling the need to hide, and the more I processed it, the more seen I could allow myself to be. The more I could just BE...

This is where the FIRE comes in.

The FIRE tool:

F ~ Face the experience: Begin by acknowledging and facing the traumatic experiences from your past. This step involves allowing yourself to recognize and accept the reality of what happened.

I ~ Investigate the emotions: Delve deeper into your emotional responses to the trauma. Explore the range of feelings you experienced then and may still be experiencing now. This step involves understanding how the trauma has affected your emotions and behaviors.

R ~ Reflect on triggers: Identify triggers that bring back memories or emotions related to the trauma. Reflect on situations, people, or circumstances that cause distress or discomfort. This step helps you recognize patterns and understand how the trauma continues to impact your life.

E ~ Empower yourself: Take proactive steps to regain control and power over your emotions and responses. This may involve seeking therapy, practicing self-care, setting boundaries, or engaging in activities that promote healing and resilience. This step focuses on empowering yourself to overcome the effects of past trauma and move forward positively.

I'm going to be with you every step of the way, cheering you on, and celebrating your bravery and courage to do this work. The fact that you're still here reading means you have hope and hope is the seed of possibility. I'm proud of you for making it this far and for being willing to go through this process. I mean that with all my heart. You are amazing and I can't wait until you see that in yourself.

Now get out your workbook and go to the "Awareness" section. Follow step-by-step until you are complete with this section. I have included a section for taking notes so you can keep everything in one place for reflection and reference.

Once you have completed the "Awareness" section in the workbook, come back here. In the next chapter, you'll read about "Acceptance" and the important role it plays in empowerment, so you can move forward in love and happiness.

See you in the workbook!

"The only way out is through"

~ Robert Frost

Step 2: Acceptance

ACCEPTANCE ~ Embracing The Fire: The next step to shifting the paradigm is acceptance. Once we have awareness, we can receive the experience and allow what is being offered as a lesson to integrate.

Why is acceptance a key link and an important next step? Well, we cannot move forward while rejecting something that happened in our lives. Trying to Ignore a painful experience that is holding you back is like ignoring a slow leak on a boat. At first, it may seem manageable, hardly noticeable even. You might convince yourself that it's not worth the hassle to address it, especially when the sea seems calm. However, just like the leak, the effects of the painful experience gradually worsen over time, slowly eroding your sense of stability and security.

As you continue to ignore it, the leak persists, eventually leading to a point where the boat's integrity is compromised. Similarly, by avoiding confronting and processing your painful experiences, you risk undermining your emotional well-being and stability. What started as a minor inconvenience grows into a significant threat, potentially sinking your ability to navigate life's challenges effectively.

Addressing the leak requires acknowledging its existence, locating its source, and taking deliberate action to repair it. Similarly, confronting and addressing painful experiences involves acknowledging their impact, understanding their origins, and actively engaging in healing and self-care. Just as repairing the leak strengthens the boat's resilience, confronting painful experiences empowers you to build resilience and move forward with greater strength and clarity.

If you don't, then you must change your life to work around avoiding water.

Now think about this in relation to fire. If people had avoided fire and not accepted it, and the purpose it serves in our lives, then we never would have learned how to use fire to our advantage. People die from fire all the time, and we don't reject fire because we are aware of its power. Both the positive and the negative that are associated with it, we accept all that comes with it, so we can use it to live. Our painful experiences are no different.

Awareness of our painful experiences and the impact they have on our life allows us to process the meaning, lessons, messages, and on. It allows acceptance of them into our lives and lived experience, so we can learn, grow and build. If we keep rejecting, not accepting, what we now know, we remain stuck in a victim-mindset and reject anything good that comes with the bad. It's a place people get stuck, and they often either shut down into a depressed and withdrawn space or repeat their story to everyone. All. Of. The. Time...

I experienced this after the loss of my first son, Rylan. I somehow believed that accepting my experience meant I wasn't a "good" mom. Mom-guilt is so weird. This extended to the point that it was hard for me to leave the cemetery when visiting them because I was leaving my baby outside in the rain and cold. I felt overtaken by the need to talk about it. My heart was trying so hard to reconcile all the pain, so I could let it go. However, I was rejecting the lessons, the experience, the messages, the meaning and, along with it, I was rejecting healing, so I couldn't let it go. It kept repeating like a loop and guess what happened? One year later, I experienced the loss all over again when I lost my second son, Kearnan.

During this season of my life, a dear friend lost her baby after a traumatic delivery and because I was holding onto my pain, it was as if my babies had died all over again. I wanted so desperately to keep her from feeling this pain because I loved her and knew how deeply it hurt. I felt in my heart if I could heal her pain, mine would have a purpose. What I didn't realize was that by not accepting the loss of my son's, I wasn't much help to anyone. This is how the rejection of my experience kept looping them back into my life in a disempowering way.

I was an absolute mess and miserable to be around while I fought to put one foot in front of the other. The support I needed during this time was tremendous. Looking back, I see how I was absolutely the weakest link during this time. I had awareness of all that had happened and how it all played into my life, and I just couldn't accept it. I held it as far away as I could while holding my nose, trying to ignore what I knew, just like dog poop. You can only hold dog poop for so long before you're forced to do something with it.

As I learned and grew more, I shifted and started accepting parts of my experience, and continued to reject others. I finally accepted the loss of my son's, and I finally had my baby, and I still hadn't accepted the loss of my fertility, creating another learning opportunity for myself. A traumatic surrogacy experience where it felt like my child had been kidnapped, I couldn't experience the pregnancy, know how he was or be at his delivery. This was all created by my rejecting the loss of my uterus and not being able to experience delivering my babies. There were compounding lessons I wasn't even aware of at the time and I will go into those details later. You see how the universe creates with us the lessons we refuse to accept? The hardest part is we hurt those around us even though we don't intend to.

I remember a client who had been raped when she was a teenager. She had great awareness about the experience and the impact on her life. The way it was holding her back from relationships, advancing in her career and even how it caused her to disconnect with her family. She even knew the lessons and meaning of the experience and why it happened, and she was pushing it all away. She couldn't integrate the experience into her life because she couldn't accept the entire experience. So, guess what lessons she was getting on loop? Lessons that involved her boundaries at work, in dating, in her family and with her friends. She was walking around, always feeling violated and out of control of her boundaries.

Once I started working with her on how to shift into acceptance and embrace the experience, accept it all, the good, the bad and the ugly, she bloomed! Not only did she regain close connection with her family, she got a promotion and met a partner who was her ideal match from her vision board! Once she embraced the lessons about the experience and boundaries, she could be clear about her boundaries and expectations in all areas of her life. Now her employer knew that in order to keep her what she needed, her family knew where the lines were, and she could say "no" to men who weren't right for her. This narrowed the scope to the ones who were.

Are you ready for the next section of the workbook to move into acceptance?

Let's do this!

I will walk you through each step and explain the process. Be sure to answer all the questions I guide you through. This part seems scarier than it is, and as you work through it, you will start feeling empowered again. This will get you ready to create an action plan in the next section, and I'm so excited for you! Look at how far you have come on your journey and acknowledge yourself for being brave enough to get here. I'm sending you so much love and healing as you walk into your new life and the new you.

I'll be seeing you back here once you have completed this step in the workbook.

Go get 'em tiger!

"A goal without an action plan is a daydream."

~ Nathaniel Drucker

Step 3: Action Plan

ACTION PLAN ~ Being Built: Now that you're through the FIRE, let's get you FORGED! This is an important next step in the forging process. When the metal has been in the fire long enough, it gets to just the right temperature and it's ready to be forged. If you don't know what to do with this molten metal when you pull it out of the fire, then you can't guide what it becomes. If you don't guide what it becomes, it will keep needing to repeat the first two steps. When the metal hasn't been forged yet, it's easier to repeat the first steps. Once it's forged, those lessons are ready to be locked in and the metal is stronger.

Do you recall when I talked about losing my best friend to suicide? Well, because I didn't have an action plan on how to get forged or know that I even needed to. I had a huge landslide when she died and reverted to protecting myself from the pain by avoiding and being distracted from it. I couldn't move forward into acceptance because I was stuck in "I don't know" land. This led to me re-experiencing her loss through not being included in important grieving work, helping, and gatherings. It even led to me losing a friend because I couldn't grieve her loss. I wasn't aware I was avoiding the fire. By avoiding the fire, I couldn't have awareness regarding her loss or shift into acceptance that she was really gone. I was stuck so badly...it was excruciating and devastating in so many ways.

The shining light that got me on track was my amazing friend, Sonia, who does coaching and energy work. She taught me how to make an action plan through her work. This helped me in the forging process to shape what I was to become, so I could have true forward progress. I have since been able to work through the loss of my sweet friend. However, I don't know if I will ever be able to reconcile the friendship my grief cost me. I have done this process to gain peace regarding that loss as well, so I'm not reliving that experience in my life.

A client of mine was on his third divorce. He couldn't understand why his marriages kept failing. He had done some great work and had counseling, so he could reach acceptance regarding his first two marriages. What he didn't have or know he needed was an action plan, so he could shape himself for his new life using his lived experience. He kept taking himself out of the fire with no idea what to do next. Once he started learning about the shaping process, and had a plan for how to do that, he was ready to go through the forge. This had such a profound impact on how he handled his divorce that they never completed it! They are both blissfully married to this day. He got to mold himself into his new shape, so he interacted with everything that was happening completely differently. He saw his responsibility and wasn't blaming anyone, including himself; then handled himself and his partner with compassion because that was who he was the whole time.

This part is so important and so exciting. You get to decide who you want to grow into, how to build yourself. You get to decide on a more knowledgeable, happier, more loving version of you. As you shape the new you out of your precious lived experiences, those experiences now become your driving force toward your greatness. Knowing where you've been allows you to put up navigation for the future by adding it to your form during forging. It's like adding a ring where you know you might need to tie some rope for pulling or some other tool to help you in situations that can be challenging.

No one else on this planet has your experience, through your lenses, with your mind or with your heart. What you do with an experience you have learned and grown from is your legacy, your impact on this planet, and the lives of everyone around you. Isn't that just amazing? I'm truly in awe every time I get to witness people coming out on the other side of their experiences, like being reborn. I'm blessed to be a part of it, and blessed you are reading this, that you are doing your work, that you exist and get to have your impact on this world. It's hard to fully express in words how much it means to me you are here and have reached this place in your life and in your journey.

Let's get this whole forging process going!

Go to your workbook and work on the Action Plan section. This isn't a time to rush. You are making some incredibly important decisions about how you want to build yourself, so you get to make a plan. Take in the questions, answer them from your heart, and reflect on them with your heart. Don't rush your plan, and don't forget about your "hot" ready to shape self, otherwise you will cool down in the shape of whatever you pulled out and need to start over. That's not good for anyone, especially for you.

I can't wait to see what you forge your new self into!

See you in the next section when you're ready to be anchored!

"It is not how much we do, but how much love we put in the doing."

~ Mother Teresa

Step 4: Anchoring

ANCHORING ~ Locking In What You Built: OMG! Look at the new you! How excited are you to lock this in? This is the last critical step in the Forged Method. Once the metal has been forged, it must go through a cooling process to lock the new shape. During this time, be very aware of anything that might change the shape you made. Things like old thoughts and patterns can sneak in and change things to make a spot for them to return to. Our old thoughts, patterns, and beliefs are strong. They have been around most of your life, so changing them is a sort of death they fight. Stay aware and repair those spots right away because you have time to keep them from being permanent.

Put more love and BEing here, it's not really about the DOing. We are human BEings not human DOings. Everything here should allow you to BE.

Check in with your new shape frequently, and monitor what's affecting it, and what's interacting with it during this delicate period. This is a time to be relentless about self-care, mediation, and shifting thoughts that drift to the old negative patterns. Focusing on what you envision for your life, not what you have experienced. You attract and create what you focus on, so focus on what you want and don't take up space with what you don't. The new shape you build is to attract and build the life, business, relationships, and you of your dreams. Protect this new shape as if your life depends on it, because it does.

I was unaware of any anchoring process or just how easily the old can creep in. How this played out in my life was that unworthiness and fear kept getting locked into the new me, sneaky little creeps, and I wouldn't make progress on my goals. In fact, I would continue to create debt and jobs that didn't value me because those creeps would take over. Since my shape wasn't exactly what I thought I made it to be, it was easy to get hijacked. I didn't notice them find their way in, so I never knew to fix them before I cooled.

I saw this with a coach of mine who had done this amazing transformation program and didn't cool in her new shape as she made it. What my experience ended up being was dealing with her old parts that crept in. This was a good thing for me to experience, so I could bring awareness, acceptance, and create an action plan to know how to anchor, and that anchoring was a thing. A very important thing.

I know this sounds incredibly stressful and believe me, when I figured out what happened and what I needed to do, I was worried and stressed. I was freaking out over every negative thought that flashed across my mind. It was as if my negative thoughts were whack a mole, and I needed to hit them as soon as they appeared, or I would become the mole. Well, it's not that extreme, and as humans, our primal response is to make mountains out of molehills. This is because the primal part of our brain is trying to make sure we survive, so nearly everything equals death in our primal brain. Part of the Forged Method is how to cool down exactly how you forged yourself and have grace with yourself during the process.

Part of holding this new shape is being loving, kind and patient with yourself. You get to be your own best friend to help you get to your next level and when you're ready, work on your next layer of healing.

We all fall down, it's the getting back up that defines us and builds us. You have come this far which means you can go the full distance, going through it was the hardest part of the battle and you're on the other side.

This is your practice arena so keep trying, keep practicing. It's no different from when you were a toddler and learning how to walk. We fall down so much and walk so awkwardly, and no one ever said "you know this walking thing isn't working out for you, so you should just keep crawling". Yet, as we grow up that's the message we get about everything we practice. Do not let perfection be the enemy of good or of progress. Progress and practice, not perfection, will lead you to your best life. Being the turtle is perfectly fine here, just keep moving.

Let's get this cool down on the right track. Go to the workbook and start on this section. I will walk you through how to manage the cooling process so you can anchor your new shape without those little creeps getting involved. This is also where a lot of those resources I included at the end of this book come in super handy, so you cool down the right way.

I can't wait for you to get cool! I kid, I kid, you're already cool, and your new shape gets to be cool too!

I will see you back here as we finish things up with the new, cool, anchored in you!

"Maybe you have to know the darkness before you can appreciate the light."

~ Madeline L'Engle

Putting It All Together

It takes strength, courage, and bravery to do this work, to look within, to be this vulnerable, to see where we can do better, and to create change. This process isn't linear as we trial and error what works for us and what doesn't. The tools and workbook were designed so you can find your own answers and create your own shape because "...There is no one alive that is Youer than You." ~ Dr. Seuss

When we look at transformation, the process is like peeling back the layers of an onion, and it never "ends". You will get efficient and comfortable with the process, and it will go on for the rest of your life. This may sound daunting; it's quite beautiful, really. The core of who we are will remain, and as we experience new things, learn, and grow, our beliefs, thought processes, and values will shift to become what we decide. Therefore, what we feed our minds and say to ourselves is so important. We are the outward expression of our mind's health, so if it's struggling? Then we are too. Our mind and heart work together, they are not separate. Working on one and not the other will not serve anyone, least of all yourself. Healing our heart and our mind together, and being aware of the connection, is vital in effective transformation.

As we continue being lifelong learners and growth-minders, you will uncover other things you couldn't see because of what was covering it. Once you notice this, you start the process to work on the next layer. Listen to the messages and lessons the universe gives you. They may not be obvious, and you may not understand them until much later, and that's okay. It's important to acknowledge them, question them and interact with them.

An example: Recently someone I love very much did a transformation program. I sent a message to the universe. "What would it take for *** to have the transformation... needed for their highest and greatest good?. I believe in the universe and the angels. Anything standing in the way of this, I want to uncreate and delete it. This or something better.". I use this all the time and it amazes me how the universe delivers. Well, the universe delivered, creating multiple stress factors to heighten their experience. You must melt before you can reshape and melt, they did.... The added stress opens doors that cause breakdown, and breakdown allows space for surrender, for growth, and forging.

We often see obstacles, unfortunate events, etc. with us as the victims of circumstance. What if we look at how this is happening FOR us? I struggled to do this for a long time, especially with the loss of my sons, my uterus and the pile of debt. Feeling like such a victim for years, and I'm not. A few years before I started writing this book, I started learning the difference. At this moment I don't know the full depth of the meaning regarding the car accident, loss of my sons', my uterus, fertility, or the financial burden that was left to me. The difference is now I trust it will be revealed to me in due time. I know the universe was telling me my path, and I was blatantly ignoring it for so long.

In reflection, with my newfound understanding, I now know I wasn't meant to spend my life with my ex. I was given every red flag you could think of, and I was loyal to a fault and did what I could to make him happy. I didn't know then that wasn't my responsibility, and I tried desperately, for nearly two decades, to do that. After the car accident, I was shocked back to life, both literally and figuratively. I continued trying to make him happy. However, I finally started doing things I loved that he never supported or participated in. I realized I had been living my life for him and the only thing I wanted was to be a mother and live a life with purpose. His exact words to me were, "The only reason we are doing the surrogacy is because I know you want a baby." Why did I continue? I was ignorant and didn't know what I didn't know, and definitely not listening to the flags. There are a million reasons a seventeen-year-old should never decide, or be allowed, to get married. I didn't know any better. I didn't know the cycle I was stuck in, and I didn't know there was a way for me to learn from this, so I stayed stuck.

I changed, I learned, I grew, and he wanted none of it. I was finally growing up and taking back control of myself. He wanted the kid version of me that only did what he wanted, where he had complete control and my world revolved around him. We weren't right for each other from the start, and I see it so clearly now. I was just a child, who thought I was grown up, and willing to fit myself in whatever box he wanted me in. Looking back, it makes complete sense now. When I started standing up for myself, setting boundaries, doing things I loved and no longer holding responsibility for his happiness; I no longer worked for him. I was still willing to do counseling and for us to grow together, and he told me, "I want you to stop trying. The only reason we are still married is because you keep trying and I want you to stop trying." In that moment, those words transformed me. It was like a switch had been flipped and I finally listened to the universe and let him go. That moment and those words made me realize I deserved better. It took me a long time to be thankful, as I was so incredibly sad and felt so betrayed. He just gave up because he didn't want to grow. Now I know this was exactly the wake-up call and lesson I needed to live my best life, and I am so thankful. Otherwise, I would still be the only reason we were still married, I would still be trying, and I needed to stop trying.

Do you see how the lessons and messages are not always revealed to you right away? Going through the Forged Method helps reveal what we pretend not to know. I knew these things in my heart, but my mind and heart weren't listening to each other. As woman, we are often told not to listen to our heart, our intuition, and men, often, are raised ignoring it all together. I went through lessons to teach me how to connect them so that I could be here now to serve others. My whole life I have loved helping people to be better than when I found them. This is why nursing has been such a huge part of my purpose. My heart was calling for something bigger and I went on a journey to help more people.

I know with absolute certainty I have climbed these mountains to help others climb them faster and more efficiently. To help others not feel alone. I'm listening and on the right path. I feel it in my veins! This is for those of you have seen Invader Zim or would like a moment of comedy. "Invader's blood marches through my veins like giant radioactive rubber pants! The pants command me! Do not ignore my veins!" Watch the clip, watch the whole cartoon for that matter. You're welcome in advance!

Everything's just falling into place effortlessly now that I'm no longer fighting against the universe and my purpose. I was making my life so hard for so long, and I'm thankful for the clarity I have gifted myself with those experiences. I'm not thankful my sons are gone, or that I don't currently have a uterus. I am thankful for the lessons and growth from the experiences I have lived through. My sons are loved and thought of every single day and I'm so thankful I'm their mommy, and they chose me. Without these experiences I wouldn't have my son and husband now and I wouldn't want a life that didn't have them, they are the best!

You have your own journey that you are co-creating with the universe to learn the lessons to live your best life. The Forged Method will help you gain clarity sooner so you can listen to the messages being sent to you. I don't want anyone else to struggle or to take years and many hard lessons to gain clarity for their best life. I want everyone to have it as soon as possible. If you have made it here, know it's a message from the universe that you are ready, and now is your time. You matter, the impact you are meant to have on this earth, on the people around you and beyond, in this life, matters. I can't wait to see everything you are about to do with the tools you now have and the new you out in the world!

I will mention this as I'm still working on holding my shape around this in my own cooling process. The interactions and reactions you receive from others are a message to you, not about you. We bring the exact experiences and interactions for us to grow. If something you feel is negative, investigate it. Be curious. There is a "why" and it may take time and healing to find it, know it's there. I have never accepted the saying "Everything happens for a reason". It's disempowering and creates a false narrative that things happen to us, and we are powerless against this invisible force. It also places a shame for the person experiencing the "everything happening" if they can't see the "reason" through the dark place they're in. As if they are doing sadness or grief wrong somehow. We get to find meaning and purpose through everything that happens, that is our power and our choice. This is a journey, and we take it one step at a time. We are not victims, we are champions, warriors, survivors and fighters. We get to be sad, angry; we get to feel as long as we don't unpack and live there. I love who I've become and who I'm growing to be because I have fought to be her. I'm surrounded by powerful humans who have forged themselves through the fire. We are not alone even if our experience itself is unique.

I don't believe everything happens for a reason. I do believe we can find meaning, create value, learn and grow through every experience which we face, no matter how tragic or bleak it is. We are in charge of who we are, who we become and our outcome, even if it takes time to get there. Don't ever compare your experience to anyone else's. We are all fighting our own battles, and there is no comparison. None of us can live each other's experiences or fight each other's battles. These experiences are uniquely ours for our own growth, so the difficulty is like comparing equity to equality. Everyone's painful experiences are equally painful while we go through them. None are equitable, no one is given a different amount of pain from their experience just because the experiences are different. We can all understand deep pain because being human comes with suffering so long as we are living. Have grace with others and yourself. Hold no guilt, no blame, no judgment, and no shame for yourself or others, because we are all doing the best we can with the tools we have...which are not equitable or equal.

Always find a way to leave others better than when you found them. Be a blessing in your own life and the lives of others by loving YOU and sharing YOU. You have been brought to, and through, your experiences to learn, grow and create the way only you can. BE the light for others to navigate the darkness and BEcome the light themselves.

Don't underestimate your strength and power to take charge of the direction you are going, and the life you choose to live. It doesn't mean we won't continue to go through challenges or have suffering. It does mean we own who we are through it, at the end of it, and in the future. As humans, we can trap ourselves in the victim-mindset game and compare to others, so we don't accept our own power to transform who and where we are in life. We tell ourselves that how we have it is so much harder/worse because, "insert the story we tell ourselves here". We make this so believable because it's easier than seeing the part we are playing in the life we have created. If I say something is happening to me, I don't have to think about how I am responsible for it or for fixing it. It doesn't mean what I'm going through is easy or doesn't hurt, nor does it mean resolution will come quickly. It does mean I am in charge of understanding the part I played in creating the situation I'm in and that I'm in charge of the outcome. It's like having to clean up dog poop. We can be upset about it all we want, and we still get to clean it up. We control the attitude we clean it up with and end up with after we're done cleaning.

"Do the best you can until you know better. Then when you know better, do better."

~ Maya Angelou

I will cover what to do next in the next section, so buckle up for the ride to get even more exceptional! Also, you don't have to keep your arms in on this ride, wave them all over as much as you want. Almost like the wackie inflatable arm guy at the car dealerships, the one who's always so excited!

"Be relentless about yourself and creating your best life!"

~ D'Leene DeBoer

What To Do Next

Here's the thing. You can go through all of this, do all of this work, and then get comfortable and settle. Guess what? The ego employs comfort as a strategy to gradually draw you back, not to push you forward. Before you know it, you're in a cycle you didn't see you were creating. Get comfortable being uncomfortable, pushing your own boundaries, and growing. Think of the growing pains you had as a kid. Pain is the ride or die for growth. We are developing a new habit here, so it takes practice and dedication. Don't give up on you. Don't give up on your dreams and don't settle for mediocre because you didn't wake up to be mediocre.

Start creating additional evidence to support and reinforce new habits and ways of living. One is noticing when something is uncomfortable or has a great level of difficulty. You can consciously reassure yourself that's where growth lives and intentionally seek out or lean into those moments. This doesn't mean ignoring intuition or safety concerns. Evaluate those things and seek counsel on if you're creating problems that don't exist in order to avoid them or if there are valid concerns not to proceed. Stretch where you can even when you don't want to. It may be exactly what you need.

On my website, www.dleenedeboer.com, I share many resources, upcoming workshops, conferences, etc. You can sign up for my newsletter and subscribe to my YouTube and TikTok depending on your preference. I have other platforms I use as well to make it easy for people to get the information they need. Whatever you do keep learning, growing and seeking out information from others who have been there. If someone is doing the thing you want to be doing learn from them. Invest in yourself through coaching. I wish I had known earlier in my life the benefits. I have always multiplied any coaching investment back to myself because I started doing things differently. Don't take away years of opportunity from yourself by being afraid to invest in coaching and in yourself. You are worth investing in you! My coaching has been more valuable than my degree and that is not even close to a joke or exaggeration.

I look forward to hearing from you! Please leave a review or send me a message, so I can hear about what helped you and what you've learned. I want to know your experience. If any resource has been helpful for you please comment, like and share with others so everyone gets to grow and move forward. No one gets through anything alone. We have others lifting us up even when we don't know they are.

BE the light!

"Love life. Engage in it. Give it all you've got. Love it with a passion because life truly does give back, many times over, what you put into it."

~ Maya Angelou

Live Your Best Life

You get to decide who you BE and where you're going in this life. We can't control what happens as we live our human experience, we can control how we handle what happens. We get to choose to make things a benefit to us and our lives. Is this easier said than done? Yes, and we can keep practicing and improving. When I catch myself slipping back I immediately turn it around and know that's not the path I want to return to. There's no guilt, no blame, no judgment, no shame. Just a notice moment, I make a choice about how I want to move forward and I move forward. No one is perfect and slipping back isn't a failure. Nothing is a failure if we learn and grow from it.

Every morning when you wake up make a decision about how you want to show up and experience your day. Think about a daily goal like, "At the end of the day I will look at my wins and feel accomplished." At the end of the day look at your wins, look at what you're grateful for, count your blessings big and small, especially the small. We can tend to overlook what a blessing it is to enjoy a cup of coffee, drive in our car, buy food or pay a bill. If we can't be grateful for these things how will we call in more? The little things matter.

Find ways to brighten someones day. I'm not good about verbalizing compliments to people, especially appearance, so I often say nothing. I make it a point to avoid appearance because I think it takes away from finding value in the person, and I know how important it is for people to be verbally acknowledged. Knowing this about myself, I make it a point to verbally compliment a minimum of 3 people every day I don't know. The smile on people's faces when you give them a genuine compliment is such a gift to both of you. I have had multiple times when they have told me how much they needed that and it made their day. Be a gift to others and it is also a gift to yourself.

You are your own powerhouse, so hold your head high and shine bright. People who live in darkness may find you too bright and intimidating, and that's not for you to manage. They are responsible for themselves, just as you are yourself. Have a good network of people who can give you honest feedback and pay attention to if you keep hearing the same feedback from others. A trend is worth your time to reflect on. A mean spirited, one off comment is not worth your energy. If someone is trying to drag you down or back, then evaluate that relationship. Some people cannot be in our close circle forever. I have many core friends and family who are honest and have never tried to drag me down and only lift me up. I trust their feedback. There have been plenty of others that didn't like me feeling good about myself and wanted me to stay broken. Those people are no longer a part of my life, and they are still in the same cycle which really breaks my heart. Only they can make changes to turn things around, so I had to walk away. I hold only love for them and I love myself enough to love them from a distance.

I will leave you with reminders I use and have used that have been so helpful in turning things around. There is also a list of resources in the back of this book. I consume a lot of books every year and the library, which has digital rentals as well, it is a great resource on a tight budget. Books save lives and lead to better lives, so thank you for helping support such a profound resource. Know that I'm rooting for you and so excited for you to be an empowered and powerful force in this world. We need women to be the leaders they are and men to show their leadership through vulnerability. Thank you for sharing this journey with me and so much love to you.

Some helpful reminders I use and hope they are helpful to you as well:

- No one is responsible for your mood or happiness. Don't ever hand over your power like that. You are not responsible for anyone else's either; they are.

- Be 100% responsible. No one can take responsibility. We are all 100% responsible for the part we play and own that. Look at every single situation and see the part you play in it because you can't control others, you can only control yourself, so don't focus on them.

- Always assume good intent. This doesn't mean harm isn't caused or that you ignore red flags. It means that you're not making up a story about it that creates drama.

- Don't create problems that aren't there.

- Don't take things personally.

- Every situation is neutral. We give it meaning. Take a step back and look at it without the emotions.

- No guilt, no blame, no judgment, no shame. Feedback is neutral, so do a self-check if these are present.

- We don't see situations and people as they are. We see them as we are. It's an opportunity for self-reflection and looking at what the brain could be hiding in plain sight. Treat it like a blind spot finder.

- Hurt people, hurt people. This is true for ourselves as much as it is for others.

- If you're feeling like you don't understand "why", ask yourself "What am I pretending not to know?"

- You can either be a victim or a warrior, not both. Have your time to process it and then decide the direction you are going. Honoring your experiences doesn't mean living in them.

- Start each day with gratitude, it will transform you and your life in ways nothing else can and you will see a difference quickly.

- Look for the lesson in situations that are difficult. You may not understand right away, and asking the questions allows you to see when the answer does arrive.

- Track your wins!

- Start paying attention to your language. Replace words like "have/need to" with "get to". Examples "I get to wake up early and work out; I get to pay my bills." This helps change our mindset. Also, replace the word "but" with "and". "But" takes away anything that was said before it while "and" includes it. Start having both/and.

- Find ways to stretch out of your comfort zone, especially when an opportunity to do so arises.

- Remember, everyone is doing the best they can with the tools they have. Have grace for them and especially for yourself.

- BE the light for others to navigate the darkness. It takes a village, so be that village as often as you can.

"Knowledge is power. Knowledge shared is power multiplied."

~ Robert Boyce

Resources

These are resources I have used or still use to this day and I'm happy to share them with anyone. The coaches I list here, I fully recommend and support. They did not ask me to promote them, and I asked them for permission to recommend them and share their information.

Obviously, I really want to work with you. I want to meet you and I want to know who you are, and maybe you're not feeling ready to work with me yet and that's okay. I'm a tremendous supporter of learning from different people and seeing what works well for you. The moment a teacher, coach, etc. tells you or leads you to believe no one knows better or can help you besides them. Well, that is the moment you know you're being gaslit for your money. I will add that you should finish the program you started before moving to the next, otherwise, you are leaving opportunities on the table. When someone creates a program, all the parts work together, so if you leave without completing all parts, then you won't get the full benefits. Don't do that to yourself and don't think a coach or program isn't right for you if you haven't done the work.

I consumed every free resource I could because I didn't have the money to invest in coaching. If you are struggling with finances, it's all the more reason to do this work and seek guidance with your struggles. Seeking coaching was the best decision and I wish I had known earlier in my life because I could have saved myself precious time and struggle.

Please like and share, leave reviews so others have guidance when they want to know who's right for them. Reviews benefit everyone and it doesn't cost a thing. Much love and happy journey to you and please connect with me because I want to know what has been helpful to you!

Meditations and Mindfulness:

- 5 Minute Guided Morning Meditation for Positive Energy: https://youtu.be/j734gLbQFbU

- 10 Minute Morning Meditation - High Frequency Positive Energy to Start Your Day: https://youtu.be/QtRrDrf5uSQ

- Couples Who Dance: www.youtube.com/@coupleswhodance

- Forged Through The Fire: www.youtube.com/@ForgedThroughTheFire

- Growth Training Part One with Dave Scatchard:
  https://youtu.be/x9ixjdaJAh0

- Morning Meditation for Abundance and Gratitude |
  Mindful Movement: https://youtu.be/YejV-bnt608

- Positive Morning Affirmations (Self Love,
  Abundance, Gratitude, Joy):
  https://youtu.be/QudqAIVBVr8

- Positive Morning Affirmations for Success &
  Alignment   Powerful Guided Meditation:
  https://youtu.be/tu1jk4li8YY

- Surpass Your Limits Mentor:
  www.youtube.com/@surpassyourlimitsmentor

- Sleep Hypnosis for Clearing Subconscious Negativity:
  https://youtu.be/_MCXtMjaJXw

- The Energy Queen:
  www.youtube.com/@sarahashleywheeler

Books:

- *Change Your Questions, Change Your Life* ~ Marilee
  G. Adams, PhD

- *The Universe Has Your Back* ~ Gabrielle Bernstein

- *Braving the Wilderness* ~ Brené Brown

- *Dare to Lead* ~ Brené Brown

- *I Hope I Screw This Up* ~ Kyle Cease

- *Gorilla Mindset* ~ Mike Cernovich

- *Atomic Habits* ~ James Clear

- *Good to Great* ~ Jim Collins

- *...And So, We Dance* ~ James and D'Leene DeBoer

- *Can't Hurt Me* ~ David Goggins

- *Relentless* ~ Tim S. Grover

- *Crush Your Kryptonite* ~ Nate Hambrick

- *Willpower Doesn't Work* ~ Benjamin Hardy

- *The Obstacle Is the Way* ~ Ryan Holiday

- *Girl, Wash Your Face* ~ Rachel Hollis

- *Sis, Don't Settle* ~ Faith Jenkins

- *Don't Settle* ~ Molly King

- *The Anomaly Mind-Set* ~ Sandi Krakowski

- *The Attraction Distraction* ~ Sonia M. Miller

- *The 5 Second Rule* ~ Mel Robbins

- *The Four Agreements* ~ Don Miguel Ruiz

- *The Clarity Cleans* ~ Habib Sadeghi, DO

- *The Comeback* ~ Dave Scatchard

- *You Are a Badass* ~ Jen Sincero

- *The Untethered Soul* ~ Michael A. Singer

- *Leadership and Self-Deception* ~ The Arbinger Institute

- *The Body Keeps the Score* ~ Dr. Bessel A. van der Kolk

- *Extreme Ownership* ~ Jocko Willink and Leif Babin

- *Adult Children of Alcoholics* ~ Dr. Janet Geringer Woititz

Coaches:

- <u>Jackie Bishofsky</u>
    www.growwithjackieb.com

- <u>Rebecca Blust</u>
    www.freedomforlifeinc.com

- <u>D'Leene DeBoer</u>
    www.dleenedeboer.com

- <u>James and D'Leene DeBoer of Couples Who Dance</u>
    www.coupleswhodance.com

- <u>Joshua Ludlam</u>
  www.exponentialevolution.com

- <u>Cheryl Lyons</u>
  www.visiontoaction.org

- <u>Sonia M. Miller</u>
  www.surpassyourlimits.com

- <u>Dave Skatchard</u>
  www.allstarcoaching.com

- <u>Kyle and Ariel Tresch of Couplepreneurs</u>
  www.kyleandariel.com

- <u>Sarah Ashley Wheeler</u>
  www.tiktok.com/@theenergyqueen/live

- <u>Amy Yamada</u>
  www.amyyamada.com

"...and so she danced."

~ D'Leene DeBoer

www.ingramcontent.com/pod-product-compliance
Lightning Source LLC
Chambersburg PA
CBHW060413050426
42449CB00009B/1961